Great Freezer Recipes for the Busy Household

How to Pre-Prepare Healthy Meals for the Family

Melinda Johnson

This book is dedicated to my loving family who inspired me to create this book.

Speedy Publishing LLC (c) 2014
40 E. Main St., #1156
Newark, DE 19711
www.speedypublishing.co

Ordering Information:
Quantity sales; Special discounts are available on quantity purchases by corporations, associations, and others. For details, contact the "Special Sales Department" at the address above.

-- 1st edition

Manufactured in the United States of America

TABLE OF CONTENTS

PUBLISHER'S NOTES

Disclaimer

This publication is intended to provide helpful and informative material. It is not intended to diagnose, treat, cure, or prevent any health problem or condition, nor is intended to replace the advice of a physician. No action should be taken solely on the contents of this book. Always consult your physician or qualified health-care professional on any matters regarding your health and before adopting any suggestions in this book or drawing inferences from it.

The author and publisher specifically disclaim all responsibility for any liability, loss or risk, personal or otherwise, which is incurred as a consequence, directly or indirectly, from the use or application of any contents of this book.

Any and all product names referenced within this book are the trademarks of their respective owners. None of these owners have sponsored, authorized, endorsed, or approved this book.

Always read all information provided by the manufacturers' product labels before using their products. The author and publisher are not responsible for claims made by manufacturers.

Print Edition 2014

CHAPTER 1: WHAT IS A FREEZER MEAL?

No Time to Eat Healthy?

Many people wonder what is happening in the world today. Why is everyone moving so fast? Where is the traffic coming from and where is everyone going in such a hurry? There is a phrase that has been out for quite a while; "Hurry, hurry, work and worry, where is everyone going and why so fast?

The rush everyone seems to be in is due to the current lifestyle and the high technology world we live in today. Moms have had to go back to work due to the economy, and families need two paychecks to make ends meet.

One problem standing out these days is the obesity problem and a lack of nutritious meals. The reliance on fast foods to get hungry bellies fed quickly is too often. When moms work eight to twelve hours per day, it leaves little time for the necessary things in life, like feeding families nutritious meals. It is too much of a challenge for moms and dads to meet this obligation.

Fast lifestyles present a number of problems for moms and dads. If moms could solve meal problems, it would be a major relief. Solving one major problem allows time to solve other fast lifestyle problems.

A Solution to Nutritious Meals When There Is No Time

One way moms can meet their families demands for nutritious meals, is to set one day aside to prepare the weeks dinners ahead of time, and freeze the meals as a whole serving or as individual servings. Get the children and husband involved in setting up a month's worth of meals. Get everyone's ideas and then shop around those ideas for lovely, fresh, and nutritious meals every day.

Many women have gone a step further to prepare one month of freezer meals ahead of time. Other women who do not have time to do a month of cooking have developed clubs of women. Woman prepares enough to share; thus, each woman takes home different dishes. Prior the women meet the month before to decide what it is that their families enjoy the most for a dinner meal.

The criteria are the meals must be nutritious and tasty and agreed upon by everyone in the club. When the woman wants to go it alone, she must set more time aside to prepare her meals ahead of time and store them in the freezer.

The criteria for nutritious meals include unprocessed, whole, organic, fresh or frozen foods, fruits and vegetables. Moms do not have to buy expensive foods in order to prepare a nutritious meal. However, if all a mom prepares is two meals per month then buying better whole or organic foods become very affordable.

Simply by bypassing processed carbohydrates or sugars, avoiding all the foods with excess sodium content and trans-fats, different family members will feel better while enjoying a variety of meals.

Foods prepared and frozen ahead of time always need to be cooked and ready to eat before freezing. Moms need to bake or cook or bake some casseroles before they freeze the meal while other food products do not require this. Moms will need to do some research on which foods are freezer friendly.

Moms are never going be at a loss of what to prepare for dinner due the immense variety of prepared ahead frozen meals, available across the internet on numerous websites. Moms will find breakfast, lunch, dinner meals and desserts to prepare ahead of time and freeze.

Another idea for moms is to cook a double batch of a dinner meal. For example, a mom who is making spaghetti for supper makes a double batch. The mom would prepare a spaghetti dinner to eat for that supper plus enough to freeze for another spaghetti dinner meal later on in the month.

Homemade frozen meals at home have all the freshest ingredients, compared with frozen meals that many times taste like cardboard. These meals also have unbelievable amounts of sodium and fat content in a frozen meal does not hold a candle to good home-cooked meals. Many find these meals overpriced lacking nutritional value.

Sometimes during the course of the month, a family may not have any need to take out a large casserole, when an individual serving works better. Families can also have the opportunity to mix and match their meals. Maybe someone is craving homemade spaghetti while mom would like stir-fry. Frozen individual homemade meal servings meet this purpose. No more will moms hear, "What's for dinner?"

Each container of frozen meals placed into the freezer needs to have a date prepared. Moms can rotate their freezer meals and add to it at the end of the month. Moms need to remember that freezer meals should not be in the freezer for more than six months.

Many moms realize a busy life should not be any excuse to forego feeding their family homemade and nutritious meals. They just have not discovered a simple solution to the problem. Once moms stock their freezer with at least a month's supply of nutritious meals, they are going to be quite relieved to know that when they arrive home after a hard day at work, a nutritious dinner can be on the table in no time.

Most of these frozen homemade meals fit well into individual foil containers with lids. The price of these foil containers are cheap. They withstand freezer temperatures and cook well in the microwave. Foil containers save even more money and are reusable.

Many moms are discovering how much time, money and frustrations frozen meals save fast lifestyle families. Most home cooked, nutritious meals freeze well. Homemade frozen meals must be used within six months. Freezer meals are a fantastic new food preparation journey.

Reasons for Frozen Dinners are to prepare nutritious meals daily. When unexpected company stops by, mom has a meal already prepared. There are days when mom is sick and does not feel like cooking, just pull out a homemade frozen meal.

Chapter 2: What Are The Benefits Of Preparing Freezer Meals?

Freezer meals are a great way to save you time, money, and stress in your everyday life; while at the same time allowing you to serve nutritious meals to your family and friends. Taking the time to plan and cook your meals ahead of time is one of the great ways to simplify your life, and free yourself up to spend more time with your family to do the things you enjoy. Having extra meals in your freezer is a simple way to help others and make your daily life a whole lot easier.

The first benefit of having freezer meals available is the time you save in overall cooking. Cooking for several recipes at the same time allows you to combine your tasks. For example, when cooking for all your ground beef meals, you can accomplish cooking 5 pounds of meat in the same time as you could be cooking one pound. Having one preparation time for each item saves you in your overall time. You chop all the onions you need, wash that dish, and you are done with that process for the month. It also saves a lot of time in the clean-up process. When you cook your meals in 1 or 2 days, you are just washing those dishes once.

On the days you eat your freezer meals, there are no cooking utensils to have to clean, as the meals have already been prepared ahead of time. You also save time in grocery shopping. As you plan out your meals, you only need to spend one day purchasing your main dish ingredients. The other perishable items that you will want for your daily meals can easily be picked up on another errand without having to spend another full day planning your meals and grocery shopping. Once you have a good plan in place for your cooking day, this can be repeated each time which further will save you time.

After all the meals have been prepared, there is no need to spend much time every day cooking in the kitchen. Simply open the freezer in the morning, remove the meal, and put it in the oven later on that day. You now have all that extra time saved for your other daily activities.

The second benefit to freezer meals is saving money. Food items can generally be purchased cheaper in bulk. When cooking many meals at once, you are able to save money by purchasing larger portions at one time. Buying large amounts of items on sale can reduce your costs even more. With today's busy schedules, parents often end up stopping to pick up fast food or other carry out meals because they have forgotten to plan the meals or don't have the time to cook.

Being able to pull a meal out of the freezer at any given time saves this extra money that is spent on these unexpected meal stops. As you plan your freezer meals, you will make a specific grocery list and only buy the necessary items for that day during your trip to the store. There is no impulsive buying which in turn saves us money in the long run. All of the purchased items will be used in the cooking of the meals with nothing going to waste.

A third benefit of having freezer meals on hand is that it saves you a lot of unnecessary stress. Much of our cooking stress comes from not planning ahead. We wonder what to cook for dinner and quickly search for a recipe, only to find that we don't have the ingredients for that recipe. Life is so much easier when we have planned our meals and know exactly what is for dinner tonight. All of us live very busy lives, and with all our kid's busy schedules we don't have to time to worry about what we will eat for dinner. Knowing we have a meal ready at home allows us to relax and enjoy our time with our children.

Another great benefit of freezer meals is that they often include better nutrition. When you take the time to plan out your meals, you are the one to decide what ingredients you want to include in the meal. You will be confident in serving healthy meals because you know what is included in the recipe. You aren't just placing some last minute store bought food on the table, but you are setting out a meal that has been thought through and prepared in a healthy way.

One final benefit of having freezer meals available at any time is that they allow you to be able to quickly help those in need. When a friend is experiencing difficult times and could use a meal, it is very convenient to be able to pull out an extra meal from the freezer and pass it on to them. If unexpected guests are in the area, there's no problem; just check out your freezer and choose that desired meal. Hospitality has never been easier.

Although it takes some initial time to plan and cook your freezer meals, the benefits far outweigh this time factor. Preparing meals ahead of time allows us to be confident that we are serving our family healthy meals. We can do this without the daily battles of figuring out what we're having for dinner. It frees us from experiencing unnecessary stress, and saves us money in the process. Without having to spend long hours in the kitchen each day, we have more time available to spend on our family and friends.

With today's convenient access to the internet, it’s easy to find the best freezer meal recipes. It's even possible to find a prepared shopping list with full meal instructions. With all the available information for make-a-head meals both online and in cookbooks, there is no reason not to start planning our freezer meals today and take advantage of all they have to offer.

Chapter 3: 10 Great Breakfast Freezer Meal Recipes

DELICIOUS PINEAPPLE MUFFINS

Ingredients:

2 6 oz. cartons of yogurt
1 large Egg
½ cup of applesauce
2/3 cup of brown sugar
1 cup of fresh pineapple chunks
2 cups of flour
2 tsp. of baking powder
½ tsp. of baking soda

Directions:

Start by setting the oven to 425 degrees; then, butter or with liners, line a muffin pan. Inside a food processer, mix in the egg and the 2 cartons of yogurt. Thoroughly pulse the ingredients together. Next, add in the brown sugar, the pineapple, and the applesauce into the yogurt mix and pulse again. Whisk together the baking powder, flour, and baking soda inside of a medium bowl.

Combine the wet and dry ingredients into the food processor and mix on a low speed until everything has well incorporated into one another. Inside of the prepared muffin pan, fill the cups with the mixture and bake for 15 minutes, until it is completely cooked through. Let the muffins cool, then put inside of Ziploc bags and put them in the freezer. When it is ready to be served, simply place them in a paper towel and microwave for 45 seconds.

A YUMMY FRENCH TOAST CASSEROLE

Ingredients:
1 loaf of cinnamon bread
5 large eggs
2/3 cups of milk
1 tbsp. of vanilla extract
2 tbsp. of sugar

Directions:
Start off my slicing the bread into even sized cubes. Next, mix all of the ingredients inside of a medium sized bowl. With a baking spray, coat a 9 by 13 baking dish and place the cubes inside of it and cover with the mixture of ingredients. Cover it completely with aluminum foil and store inside of the freezer. When it is ready to be served, set the oven at 350 degrees and cook for 40 minutes after it has been thawed, or for 1 hour if it is frozen.

BREAKFAST BURRITOS

Ingredients:
32 burrito sized tortillas
24 medium eggs
4 cans of drained and rinsed black beans
1 jar of salsa
1 chopped green pepper
1 cup of shredded cheese

Directions:
Whisk eggs in a bowl than mix with the green peppers into a pot. Cook over a medium heat, constantly stirring. Give it 2 minutes, then add in the beans, still stirring until the eggs are fully cooked. Spoon the egg mix into a tortilla and cover with a spoonful of salsa, do this to each tortilla and sprinkle with the shredded cheese. Fold and cover with plastic wrap, then place inside of a Ziploc bag and store in freezer. To serve, remove from plastic and microwave for 2 minutes.

MINI QUICHES

Ingredients:
5 oz. chopped frozen spinach
12 slices of ham
1 cup of shredded cheddar cheese
5 large Eggs
pepper

Directions:
Set oven at 375 degrees and inside of a colander, thaw out the spinach under running water, and then squeeze out to dry. With a nonstick spray, coat the muffin tin and in each cup place 1 piece of the ham. Press the ham down gently to for a cupped shape, and pour in a whisked mixture of the spinach and the other ingredients. Bake for 30 minutes, let cool, then place in Ziploc bag and place into the freezer. To serve, microwave for 2 minutes.

CORN WAFFLES

Ingredients:

½ cup of frozen corn

1 6 oz. corn muffin mix

2 tbsp. of milk

Directions:

Prepare the corn muffin mix according to the instructions found on the box, stirring in the corn and milk into the mixture. Inside of a preheated waffle iron, cook the mixture. After the cool, freeze, wrap in plastic, and place into the oven. Heat them in a toaster when ready to eat.

HASH BROWN AND BACON ROLL-UPS

Ingredients:

1 tbsp. of Oil

6 slices of cut bacon

2 cups of thawed and drained, frozen hash browns

8 large eggs

½ cup of salsa

16 small flour tortillas

1½ cups of shredded Pepper Jack cheese

Directions:

Heat olive oil inside of a large skillet at a medium heat and then brown a mixture of the hash browns and bacon until the potatoes have a crispy texture. Beat together the eggs and salsa in large bowl on the side and pour into the skillet with the bacon and potatoes. Stir occasionally until the eggs are fully cooked. Evenly spread the egg mixture into the tortillas and sprinkle with the Pepper Jack and roll them up. Place in freezer bags and stick into the freezer. Cover with paper towel and microwave for 2 minutes when ready to eat.

BLUEBERRY MUFFINS

Ingredients:

1½ cups of flour
¾ of a cup of brown sugar
½ cup of oats
¼ cup of wheat germ
1 tsp. of baking powder
1 tsp. of baking soda
¼ tsp. of salt
1 mashed banana
1 cup frozen blueberries
1 cup vanilla yogurt
1 large egg
1 tbsp. of applesauce
1 tsp. of vanilla

Directions:

Preheat oven at 350 degrees and mix all of the dry ingredients together in a bowl. Stir in all of the blueberries. Then, inside of a different bowl mix in all of the liquid ingredients, and mix everything together. Grease a muffin pan and fill the cups 2/3 full and bake for 18 minutes. Let the muffins cool, cover with plastic wrap, and place in the freezer. Remove and place the frozen muffins inside of a Ziploc bag, and put back inside of freezer. Wrap in paper towel and microwave for 45 seconds to serve.

BREAKFAST PIZZAS

Ingredients:

¼ cup of softened butter
5 oz. jar of cheese spread
½ lb. of spicy pork sausage
1 chopped onion
12 split English muffins

Directions:

Set oven at 350 degrees and in a large bowl, mix the butter and cheese spread, blending it really well. Cook the sausage crumbled in a large skillet over a medium heat with the onion, until the onion becomes tender. Pour the sausage mix into the cheese mix and then spread the mixture evenly onto the muffin halves. On a cookie sheet, bake for 15 minutes, cool, then place inside of a Ziploc bag and freeze. Microwave for 2 minutes when ready to eat.

SAUSAGE AND EGG BURRITOS

Ingredients:

½ lb. crumbled pork sausage
12 flour tortillas
6 large eggs
¼ cup of milk
1 chopped banana pepper

Directions:

Inside of a bowl, whisk the eggs, milk, banana pepper, and the sausages. Place into a large skillet and cook over a medium heat, stirring the mix constantly until the eggs cook all of the way. Spoon the mix into tortillas evenly, and roll them up. Cover in plastic and freeze. When ready to eat, microwave for 2 minutes and enjoy.

BANANA OATMEAL CUPS

Ingredients:

3 Mashed Bananas

1 Cup of Vanilla Almond Milk

2 Large Eggs

1 tbsp. of baking powder

3 cups of oats

1 tsp. of vanilla extract

3 tbsp. of mini chocolate chips

Directions:

Begin by setting the oven at 375 degrees. Inside of a bowl, mix all of the ingredients together with the exception of the chocolate chips. Set aside, and spray a muffin pan with non-stick spray. Stir the chocolate chips in the oatmeal mixture and evenly spoon into 15 cups in the muffin pan. They should fill up almost all of the way. Bake for 30 minutes and let cool. Place in Ziploc bag and store in freezer. To serve, let thaw, and microwave for 30 seconds.

Chapter 4: 10 Great Poultry And Seafood Freezer Meal Recipes

With such busy lives and hectic schedules sometimes putting a home cooked meal on the table feels like an impossible task. One of the easiest ways to eliminate the stress and frustration is to cook make-ahead meals that can be cooked when you have some free time and frozen to eat later. You can either cook multiple meals on the weekend to freeze in one large family size portion or smaller portions for individual use. Another option is to double any of these recipes and enjoy one right away while freezing the remainder for later. The "cook once and eat twice" philosophy is a huge time saver!

For all of these meals it is recommended that you use freezer safe containers and storage bags to maintain the quality of the food while freezing. Freezer safe containers help minimize freezer burn over time. Also be sure to leave a little extra space in your containers to allow for expansion as the food freezes. This will help minimize the chance of your container cracking.

JAMBALAYA

Ingredients:

1 cup chicken broth

2-3 sweet peppers (any color), chopped
1 medium onion, diced
2 cans diced tomatoes with juice
2 cloves of garlic, minced finely
1 pound of cooked and deveined shrimp, uncooked
2 cups cooked chicken, chopped coarsely
½ pound cooked sausage crumbles
1 bay leaf
2 tsp. Cajun or prepared jambalaya seasoning

Directions:
Place all ingredients in a freezer bag or container EXCEPT THE BROTH and freeze them immediately. The night before you are ready to cook thaw the ingredients. Add to slow cooker ADD BROTH and cook on low setting for 6-8 hours (high setting is not recommended).

CHICKEN AND STUFFING BAKE

Ingredients:
4 boneless, skinless chicken thighs, chopped to 2 inch pieces
1 bag frozen mixed vegetables
2 cans prepared chicken gravy
1 box of prepared stuffing, cooked according to package instructions
Salt and pepper to taste

Directions:
Add chicken, vegetables and gravy to a slow cooker and cook on low setting 8 hours or high setting 4 hours. These ingredients can also be cooked on the stovetop at medium-high heat. Simmer until chicken is cooked through. After chicken and vegetables are cooked, prepare stuffing according to package directions. In a freezer safe container, sprayed lightly with cooking spray, line the

bottom with the chicken and vegetables. Spread to a uniform layer. On top layer the cooked stuffing. Freeze.

Cooking Instructions:

Thawed the night before – Bake 350 for 25-30 minutes

From Frozen – Bake 350 for 60-75 minutes

FISH FILLET BAKE

Ingredients:

Frozen prepared fish fillets

2 cans cream of chicken soup

1 cup shredded cheddar cheese

3 cups cooked rice

Salt and pepper to taste

Directions:

Cook the rice and drain of any water. Once cooked combine with soup. Spray the bottom of a freezer safe container lightly with cooking spray. In bottom of the container place the rice and soup mixture. Place the fish fillets in the bed of rice and top with a sprinkle of cheese. Freeze.

Cooking Instructions:

Thawed the night before – Bake 350 for 25-30 minutes.

From Frozen – Bake 350 for 60-75 minutes.

CHICKEN, RICE AND GRAVY

Ingredients:

1 pound cooked, chopped chicken. A rotisserie-cooked chicken is a great way to save time.
2 cans prepared chicken gravy
3-4 cups hot cooked rice
Optional: A total of 2 cups frozen peas, green beans and/or carrots in any combination that will please your family.
Salt and pepper to taste

Directions:

On stovetop combine all ingredients in a large pot over medium-high heat and cook until the gravy is bubbly. Transfer to freezer containers. The night before you plan to eat thaw ingredients, you can heat in the microwave or stovetop until hot and bubbly.

CHICKEN TORTILLA PIE

Ingredients:

2 cups cooked, chopped chicken. A rotisserie-cooked chicken would be very flavorful.
12 soft tortillas warmed for a few seconds in the microwave
1 small can diced chilies
2 cups Verde salsa (you can use regular salsa if you prefer)
1¼ cup sour cream -set aside ¼ cup
2 cups shredded, Mexican style cheese, set aside ½ cup

Directions:

Lightly spray your freezer storage container with cooking spray. (This meal would work best in a freezer to oven safe container.) In a large bowl combine the chilies, chicken, salsa and sour cream. Place four of the warmed tortillas in the bottom of the pan. On top of the tortillas place half of the chicken mixture. Top with a sprinkle of cheese. Top with four more warmed tortillas and repeat step #3. Top with last four tortillas. Spread the ¼ cup of sour cream that was set aside on top of the tortillas. Sprinkle with the ½ cup of shredded cheese. Freeze. The night before ready to eat, thaw in the refrigerator. Bake at 375 for 30-40 minutes.

TOMATO CHICKEN

Ingredients:

2 pounds boneless, skinless chicken breast, chopped to 2" pieces
2 tbsp. butter, melted
1 can diced tomatoes
1 small can tomato paste
2 tbsp. red wine vinegar
1 tsp. each: dry basil and dry oregano
Salt and pepper to taste

Directions:

In a bowl combine butter, tomato paste and vinegar. Set aside Place chicken and diced tomatoes (with juices) in slow cooker and add seasoning. Pour liquid mixture over top and cook on low setting 8-10 hours or high setting 4-6 hours. Thaw the day before serving and serve over cooked rice or pasta.

HAWAIIAN-STYLE SWEET AND SOUR CHICKEN

Ingredients:

1 pound boneless chicken breasts or thighs, chopped
1 large can pineapple chunks, with juice
1 medium bell pepper, chopped
½ medium onion, chopped
1 cup prepared teriyaki sauce
2 tbsp. soy sauce

Directions:

Place the chicken, pineapples and vegetables in a slow cooker. In a bowl combine teriyaki sauce and soy sauce. Pour into the slow cooker. Cook on low setting 8-10 hours. Freeze. The night before serving thaw in refrigerator, either warm in microwave or in a skillet over medium-high heat for 10 minutes. Serve over rice.

BACON AND CHEESE CHICKEN

Ingredients:

6 boneless, skinless chicken thighs, coarsely chopped
10-12 pieces well cooked bacon, crumbled
¼ cup prepared teriyaki sauce
½ cup prepared ranch salad dressing
1 cup shredded cheddar or Colby cheese

Directions:

Place chicken pieces in the slow cooker. In a bowl mix sauce and salad dressing. Pour over chicken. Top with cheese and bacon and stir. Cook on low setting 6-8 hours or high setting 3-4 hours. Transfer to freezer safe container or storage bag and freeze. Thaw the night before serving.

HOMEMADE CHICKEN NUGGETS

Ingredients:

1 pound boneless chicken tenders
2 cups prepared bread crumbs (panko work great in this recipe)
1 cup crumbled cracker crumbs
2 eggs, beaten well
1 cup milk
Salt and pepper to taste
1 tsp. garlic salt

Directions:

Preheat oven to 375 degrees.

In bowl combine eggs and milk. In a second bowl combine the breadcrumbs, crackers, garlic salt and salt and pepper. For each piece of chicken dip in milk and egg mix, allow the excess to drip. Then coat in bread crumb mix. Then shake off any excess coating. Place on baking sheet that has been lightly sprayed with cooking spray. Repeat until all the chicken is breaded. Bake for 20-25 minutes until the coating is browned slightly. Allow the chicken to cool before freezing flat. Can cook thawed or from frozen like any commercial frozen chicken nuggets.

TUNA CASSEROLE

Ingredients:

2 cans tuna in water, drained of water and flaked with a fork
2 cans cream of chicken soup
2 cups shredded cheddar
2 cups cooked peas, drained of any water
1 package of egg noodles, cooked and drained
½ cup half and half
Salt and pepper to taste

Optional Crumb Topping:

1 cup bread crumbs
½ cup crumbled potato chips
¼ Olive oil

Directions:

In a large bowl combine tuna, soup, cheese and peas. Mix. Add half and half and season to taste. Combine with cooked egg noodles and place in a freezer safe container. This is a great meal to freeze in an oven ready pan so you can go straight from freezer to oven.

Optional Topping:

Combine breadcrumbs, chills and oil. Spread over top of casserole.

Cooking Instructions:

Thawed the night before – Bake 350 for 25-30 minutes.
From Frozen – Bake 350 for 60-75 minutes.

Chapter 5: 10 Great Vegetarian Freezer Meal Recipes

THE BEST FRENCH ONION SOUP

Ingredients:

10 peeled and sliced yellow onions
2 tbsp. of oil
2 tbsp. of sugar
1 tsp. of dried oregano
Salt and pepper
3 cans of vegetarian broth
3/4 cup of dried red wine

Directions:

Heat the oven to 450 degrees and inside of a big roasting pan, cook oil, sugar, onions, thyme, and pepper and salt. Use aluminum foil to cover and steam for 30 minutes. Uncover and cook for 1 more hour, stirring in 30 minute intervals. Then place this mixture into a saucepan along with the broth and 6 cups of water. Bring to a boil, and then simmer for 20 minutes. Over medium heat, pour wine into the roasting pan and simmer for 2 minutes. Let cool thoroughly before freezing.

VEGETARIAN JAMBALAYA WITH A SPICY KICK

Ingredients:

1 chopped onion
1 tbsp. of oil
1 chopped green bell pepper
1/2 cup of celery (chopped)
3 garlic cloves (minced)
2 cups of water
14 oz. can of un-drained tomatoes
8 oz. can of tomato sauce
1/8 tsp. of crushed fennel seeds
1/2 tsp. of dried Italian seasoning
1/4 tsp. of crushed red pepper flakes
1 cup of uncooked long grain rice
15 oz. can of rinsed and drained butter beans
15 oz. can of rinsed and drained red beans

Directions:

Set stove on medium and heat oil inside of a large skillet. Place in the green bell pepper, celery, onion, and garlic and cook the mixture until it is tender, generally 4 minutes. Be sure to stir the mixture frequently. Then, include the tomatoes, water, tomato sauce, fennel seed, red pepper flakes, and Italian seasoning. Bring everything into a boil and stir in the rice. Reduce the heat to low, cover the skillet, and let simmer for 30 minutes. Afterward, include the beans, and cook for 10 more minutes. Place the ingredients into a plastic freezer container then let cool in the fridge and then place container into the freezer.

DELICIOUS EGGPLANT PARMIGIANINO

Ingredients:

2 cans of peeled tomatoes
2 tbsp. of olive oil

Salt and pepper to taste
2 globe eggplants sliced 1/4 inch thick crosswise
1 cup flour
3 lightly beaten eggs
1 cup dried breadcrumbs
Vegetable oil
½ cup of grated parmesan
½ lb. of mozzarella cut into chunks

Directions:
Puree tomatoes in a process and stir in olive oil after pouring it into a medium skillet. Boil, then bring to a simmer for 30 minutes until it thickens, season with pepper and salt to taste. On the side, mix salt with eggplant in a colander and let this sit for 30 minutes. Dry the eggplants with paper towels, dip them in flour, then in the eggs, and lastly, sprinkle with the breadcrumbs. Preheat oven at 375 degrees and set a wire rack aside. Fill a large skillet half way with vegetable oil and heat at a medium-high and cook the eggplants for 3 minutes on each side, place on rack to dry. Inside of 9 by 13 baking dish, layer a cup of the tomato sauce, place half of the eggplants on top, and coat with Parmesan. Then repeat with the other half, finishing it with a top coat of the Mozzarella. Bake for 45 minutes, after cooling, freeze in correct container.

YUMMY CORN WAFFLES

Ingredients:
6 oz. corn muffin mix
½ cup of frozen corn

Directions:
Follow the package directions for the corn muffin mix, then stir corn into batter. Add an additional 2 tbsp.s of milk into the mix. Cook inside of a preheated waffle iron and freeze for a quick

breakfast any morning.

BLACK BEAN QUESADILLA

Ingredients:
15 ounces rinsed can of black beans
½ cup shredded Monterey jack cheese
¼ cup fresh salsa
8 inch whole wheat tortillas
2 tsp. of canola oil

Directions:
Inside of a bowl, combine the salsa, cheese, and beans; then, evenly spread the mix on the tortillas and fold them closed. In a nonstick skillet, heat the oil on medium. Cook quesadillas two minutes on each side until lightly browned. Wrap in foil and freeze.

SPINACH AND PARMESAN CAKES

Ingredients:
12 ounces fresh spinach
½ cup ricotta cheese
½ cup shredded parmesan
2 large beaten eggs
1 minced garlic clove
Salt and pepper

Directions:

Begin by setting the oven temperature at 400 degrees. In a food processor, pulse the spinach and then place it into a bowl. Mix in the ricotta, eggs, garlic, parmesan, and salt and pepper. Coat a 8 cup muffin pan with cooking spray and evenly divide the spinach mixture into them. Cook for 20 minutes, let cool, and then freeze in an airtight bag.

GREEN VEGGIE PIZZA

Ingredients:

1 pound pizza dough (prepared)
5 ounces of chopped arugula
¼ cup of water
2 cups broccoli (chopped)
Salt & pepper
½ cup of pesto
½ cup shredded mozzarella

Directions:

Preheat the oven at 450 degrees and coat baking sheet with an even layer of cooking spray. On a floured surface, roll the dough out and then place on baking sheet. Bake for ten minutes. In a large skillet on the stove, cook the broccoli and water on a medium heat, covered, for 3 minutes. Stir in the arugula and cook for an additional 2 minutes and then season with pepper and salt. Spread the pesto on the dough, top with the broccoli mixture, then, top that with the mozzarella. Stick into a freezer safe container and store. When it is ready to be eaten, preheat oven at 450 degrees and bake for ten minutes.

RAVIOLI, FLORENTINE STYLE

Ingredients:

20 ounce cheese ravioli (frozen)
4 minced cloves of garlic
6 tsp. of olive oil
¼ tsp. salt
16 ounce chopped spinach (frozen)
½ cup of water
¼ tsp. red pepper flakes (crushed)
¼ cup parmesan (grated)

Directions:

Prepare the ravioli in a big pot of boiling water. On the side, heat 2 tsp. of oil in a skillet. Put in the garlic then cook for 30 seconds. Add salt, red pepper, water, and spinach and cook for 7 minutes, stirring continuously. Let the ravioli cool, and place in a sealable bowl. Place in freezer, and when ready to eat, warm in pot for 5 minutes.

STRAWBERRY-RHUBARB SOUP

Ingredients:

4 cups cubed rhubarb
3 cups of water
1½ cups of sliced strawberries
¼ cup of sugar
1/8 tsp. of salt
1/3 chopped mint
Pepper

Directions:

Boil water and rhubarb in a large saucepan for about 5 minutes. Transfer it to a medium bowl and refrigerate it for 20 minutes, stirring occasionally, to let it cool. Put the rhubarb into a blender with the strawberries, salt, and sugar and blend the mix until it is smooth. Return to the bowl and mix in the mint and pepper. You can freeze the bowl and thaw when ready to serve. Serve chilled.

DELICIOUS PEA SOUP

Ingredients:

12 cups of water

2 pounds of English peas, with shells

1/3 cup of dill (finely diced)

1 tsp. of salt

¾ cup yogurt (plain)

Pepper

Directions:

Bring water to a boil in a bowl, place in peas, then return back to heat and cook for 45 minutes, stirring occasionally. Transfer peas into a food processor and blend with cooking liquid. Return the soup back to the pot and bring to a boil. After, let is simmer for 35 minutes. Let it cool and place it in a freezer safe bowl and stick it into the freezer. When ready to serve, thaw, and then warm in a pot, stirring constantly. Serve with a dollop of yogurt on top.

CHAPTER 6: 10 GREAT CHILI, STEW AND SOUP FREEZER MEAL RECIPES

I am going to share with you some of my very favorite (and most popular) soups and stews. There are many advantages of cooking soups and stews at home. The first is that a soup is an easy way to prepare an easy, healthy meal with tons of nutrition and lots of flavor. The second is that you can control the ingredients. Many canned soups are full of sodium and other ingredients you may not want in your diet. By making soup yourself you can cut all of those unwanted ingredients.

The third major benefit is that soups, stews and chili's are incredibly easy to freeze. Whether you want to freeze a large meal for a mid-week dinner or single servings these are meals that freeze and reheat beautifully. You can thaw and cook or even cook from frozen. Also keep in mind that if you double any of these recipes you can have one meal right away and freeze another for later.

For all of these recipes can freeze the prepared meal in one large or several smaller portions. You can use a freezer safe storage container or storage bag. Just be sure to use a freezer safe container or storage bag to preserve to food properly. Not all containers are equal when freezing. Also be sure to leave enough space at the top of the container so the container does not split or break.

CHILI

Ingredients:

1 can black beans, drained and rinsed
1 can kidney beans, drained and rinsed
1 can diced tomatoes, with juice
1 pound ground chicken, turkey, or beef, browned and drained
1 onion, diced
1 green pepper, seeded and chopped
2-4 tbsp. Chili Powder (depending upon how hot you like your chili)
1 tsp. dry basil
Salt and pepper to taste

Directions:

Add all ingredients to slow cooker and cook on low setting for 8-10 hours or high setting 4-6 hours.

Optional:

Serve with shredded cheese and a dollop of sour cream.

COWBOY STEW

Ingredients:
1-2 pounds stew meat or beef cubes
1 cup all-purpose flour
1/3 cup olive oil
2 large potatoes, cleaned and cubed
1 cup baby carrots
1 medium yellow onion, diced
1½ ounce can diced tomato, with juices
1½ ounce can beef broth
2 bay leaves
1 tbsp. dry thyme leaves
Salt and pepper to taste
Optional: 1 cup frozen peas and/or green beans

Directions:
Coat the beef in flour. Heat half of the olive oil in a large skillet over medium-high heat. Brown the meat in two to three shifts (be careful not to overcrowd the pan). Transfer the cooked beef to a slow cooker. Add the onions to the skillet and cook until translucent. Stir in the tomatoes and cook an additional 2-3 minutes. Transfer to slow cooker. Pour the remaining ingredients into the slow cooker, cover and cook on low setting 8-10 hours or high setting 4-6 hours. Add the frozen vegetables about thirty minutes before you are ready to serve. Be sure to remove the bay leaves before serving.

CHEESY POTATO SOUP

Ingredients:
2 cans cream of potato soup
2 cans chicken broth
4 slices of cooked and crumbled bacon
6 red potatoes, diced (you can either remove the skin or leave on)

3 tbsp. butter
3 cloves of garlic, minced
½ cup heavy cream
¼ cup flour
3 cups of whole milk
1 cup sour cream
½ cup shredded Colby cheese
¼ cup Parmesan cheese
2 Tbsp.s seasoned salt
½ tsp. pepper
1 tsp. dry parsley

Directions:
Place diced potatoes in a microwave safe dish and microwave on high for 8 minutes. Heat a large skillet over medium high heat and add the butter. Add the onion and garlic and cook until the onions are golden. Transfer to a slow cooker. In slow cooker add the onions, cooked potatoes and remaining ingredients. Wisk until well blended. Cook on low 8 hours or high 4 hours.

BROCCOLI CHEDDAR SOUP

Ingredients:
8 tbsp. butter
1 yellow onion, diced finely
1/3 cup flour
4 cups whole milk

2 cups half and half
1/3 cup sour cream
¼ tsp. nutmeg
4 heads of broccoli cut into florets
4 cups grated cheese (any combination of cheddar, Colby, jack, etc.)
1 tsp. salt
1 tsp. pepper

Directions:
Heat a pot at medium-high heat. Add the butter and cook the onions about 4-5 minutes. Sprinkle in the flour and continue cooking another minute. Add the half and half and milk to the pot. Stir. Add the nutmeg, broccoli and salt and pepper. Cover the pot and then reduce the heat to low. Simmer the soup for 25-30 minutes. Once the broccoli is tender add the cheese and let is slowly melt. You can either serve as is or you can use an immersion blender to mash some of the broccoli into the broth. (If you don't have an immersion blender you can blend half of the soup in a blender and return to pot).

HAM AND CORN CHOWDER

Ingredients:
2 cans chicken broth
2 cups whole milk or half and half
2 cans cream of celery soup
2 cans creamed corn
2 cans corn niblets
½ cup dry mashed potato flakes
3 cups ham, cooked and chopped

Directions:
Add all of the ingredients to a slow cooker and cook low 4-6 hours.

Add salt and pepper to taste and serve.

BUFFALO WING SOUP

Ingredients:
2 cups cooked and cubed chicken
½ yellow onion, diced
3 celery stalks, chopped
4 tbsp. butter
¼ cup flour
2 cups fat free or 1% milk
¾ cup chicken broth
4 ounces Velveeta cheese
1/3 to ½ cup prepared hot wing sauce
½ tsp. garlic salt

Directions:
Before chopping your chicken and vegetables heat slow cooker to high, add butter and place lid on top; while chopping allow the butter to melt. Once melted add the flour and mix well. To the slow cooker add all the ingredients and cook on low setting 6-8 hours or high setting 3-4 hours. The soup is done when the vegetables are soft.

VEGGIE SOUP

Ingredients:
1 pound ground beef, browned and drained

2 yellow potatoes, diced
1 onion, diced
2 celery stalks, chopped
1 bag frozen mixed vegetables
1 can diced tomatoes, with juice
3 cups beef broth
1 cup tomato sauce
2 bay leaves
1 tsp. each dry basil, oregano and parsley
Salt and pepper to taste

To Prepare Add all ingredients to a slow cooker and cook on low setting 8-10 hours or high setting 4-6 hours. Be sure to remove the bay leaves before serving.

WHITE BEAN CHICKEN CHILI

Ingredients:
1 can navy beans, drained and rinsed
1 can garbanzo beans, drained and rinsed
1 can diced tomatoes, with juice
1 pound ground chicken or turkey, browned and drained
1 onion, diced
1 green pepper, seeded and chopped
2-4 tbsp. Chili Powder (depending upon how hot you like your chili)
1 tsp. dry basil
Salt and pepper to taste

Directions:
Add all ingredients to slow cooker and cook on low setting for 8-10 hours or high setting 4-6 hours.

Optional:
Serve with shredded cheese and a dollup of sour cream.

CHICKEN CORN CHOWDER

Ingredients:
4 boneless, skinless chicken breasts, chopped coarsely
2 cans cream of chicken soup
1 can corn niblets
2 cups water
1 can diced tomatoes, with juice
Salt and pepper to taste

Directions:
Place all ingredients in a slow cooker and cook low setting 8-10 hours or high setting 4-6 hours.

HOMEMADE CHICKEN BROTH

Ingredients:
1 rotisserie cooked chicken
2 carrots, skinned
2 celery stalks
1 onion
Water

Directions:
Remove the meat from the rotisserie chicken and use the chicken to make another delicious soup. Place carcass in a slow cooker. (Keep in mind the more chicken you leave on the carcass the more

flavorful the broth.) Add vegetables around the carcass. Fill with enough water to just cover the entire carcass. Cook on low setting 8-10 hours or high setting 4-6 hours. Strain out the vegetables and chicken. Be careful not to leave in any chicken bones.

Chapter 7: 6 Great Dessert Freezer Meal Recipes

BANANA ICE CREAM

This good for you fruit dessert is exceptional in taste and texture. It takes about 10 minutes to make and only takes a few ingredients.

Ingredients:

2-4 tbsp. of milk
1 tsp. vanilla extract
2 frozen ripe peeled bananas (cut in chunks)

Directions:

Take your food processor, put the frozen bananas inside and puree. Add vanilla extract, a couple of spoonfuls of milk to give a soft serve texture to the ice cream. You can either serve in a stemmed parfait glass in a cone, or as a sundae with some chocolate syrup. If you are looking for extra added flavor, you can flavor the ice cream with frozen fruits that you puree with the banana. If you are a vegan but want to use this recipe, try replacing milk with juice.

ICE CREAM CAKE

This 30 minute recipe takes 5 minutes to prepare and 25 minutes to complete.

Ingredients:
1 tsp. vanilla extract (pure)
¾ cup sugar (granulated)
1 chilled cup whole milk
2 chilled cups heavy cream
2/3 cup cake mix

Directions:
Place ice cream maker bowl in the freezer. Keep there for at least 24 hours. In a medium bowl, whisk granulated sugar and milk 'til the sugar has dissolved completely. Mix in the vanilla and cream to taste. Stir your cake mix until all lumps are gone. Pour the entire mixture into the bowl and mix for 30 minutes until it becomes thicker. Remove the ice cream from the bowl and put into a medium container Place ice cream and bowl in the freezer to harden.

DOUBLE CHOCOLATE FUDGE POPS

Ingredients:
2 tbsp. of cornstarch
2 tbsp. of cocoa powder
2½ cup of milk
1 tsp. vanilla extract
1 tbsp. butter
¼ cup miniature semisweet chocolate chips
½ cup sugar

Directions:
Mix together, cocoa powder, cornstarch and milk in a saucepan over medium heat. Let the mixture simmer, stir until it becomes thick. Remove the saucepan from heat; stir in butter and vanilla extract. Pour mixture into a bowl, and refrigerator for about 20 minutes. Stir in the semisweet chocolate chips into the cooled mixture. Pour mixture into molds and freeze for 4 to 6 hours.

FROZEN BANANA POPSICLE

This is a treat that is perfect for kids and adults

Ingredients:
5 bananas (ripe)
1 cup peanuts
3 cups dark hard shell chocolate syrup
10 Popsicle sticks (wooden)

Directions:
Peel each banana and cut them in half. Insert the Popsicle sticks in each. Cover the bananas with chocolate syrup Roll bananas in the peanuts and place in freezer for 3 hours.

CREAMSICLE CUBES

If you love eating on ice, then jazz your cubes up with this simple to make freezer recipe.

Ingredients:

1 cup orange juice

1 cup Dannon light-n- fit vanilla flavored yogurt

Directions:

Fill ice trays half full with yogurt

Top off with orange juice

Freeze for at least 3 hours

STRAWBERRY POPS

A frozen treat that can't be beat, its flavor will rock your buds.

Ingredients:

1 can fat free evaporated milk

1 pint strawberry stemmed

3 tbsp. orange juice concentrate (frozen)

Directions:

Take your blender, blend ingredients together for 1 minute. Pour the mix into wax coated paper cups (eight 3 ounce cups) Place in a pan (shallow) and put in the wooden Popsicle sticks (make sure they are centered). Freeze for about four hours. Once pops are completely frozen, transfer to a releasable Ziploc bag for storage.

About the Author

Everyday Mom Melinda Johnson became a hero in her family when she started cooking amazing meals each night. Now she's widening her heroic scope by sharing nutritious and delectable dinner recipes that allow customers to create them one day and defrost and cook days, even weeks or months later.

After years of pre-packaged offerings, Melinda's youngest daughter clenched her fists and yelled, with all the drama an eight-year-old can muster, "No More Pot Pie, Mom!! It's just... gross!" Pot Pie was Melinda's favorite freezer-to-oven option after pizza, and what kid complains about pizza? Apparently her daughter had had enough of it though. After a little talk about attitude, they sat down together to talk about food, and chose a few new recipes to create from scratch. Her family loved the "real" food so much, she knew a change was necessary.

The problem was, Melinda was still just as busy. She didn't have the time to cook for hours each night. Overtime, she found that some of their favorite recipes could be made ahead of time and frozen. For years now, she's been cooking on Sunday afternoons and freezing meals for the crazy days later in the week. At the request of family and friends, she's recently created her first cookbook. She's thrilled to share her secrets with other moms who are in rut.

www.ingramcontent.com/pod-product-compliance
Ingram Content Group UK Ltd.
Pitfield, Milton Keynes, MK11 3LW, UK
UKHW021829270726
14058UKWH00001B/46